Clicker
&Target Training

Expert Guide to Motivational Training for Fun and Competition

by Angela White
Second Edition

Clicker and Target Training
Expert Guide to Motivational Training for Fun and Competition
By Angela White

Second Edition

Main photographs by
John Midgely, Hull and Mike White, Doncaster.

A record for this book is available in the British Library

ISBN 1-899057-04-8

Printed by Askew Design and Print, Doncaster.

Published by Rainbow Publishing

PO BOX 1044 HAXEY, DONCASTER. DN9 2JL.

Telephone/Fax: 01427 753918

First Published March 2000

Revised Second Edition Published March 2003

Contents

Acknowledgements

Thanks to students of canine behaviour from Bishop Burton College for giving up their time to pose for photographs. Especially Sophie Fairfax who gave up her day to help with the main photo shoot for this and other books and is our resident dog sitter when needed.

To my students in Germany for posing for the Heelwork to Music/Freestyle shots during my workshop in Germany.

To Tanja Gube for her picture of her Alaskan Malamute – Choya, holding a dumbbell.

To John Midgley for his patience in taking some excellent shots of the dogs and cat. To Carol Midgley, for the loan of Akamai Gorgeous Girl (Jazz) for some of the puppy shots.

Mike White for the balance of the photographs.

Introduction

Techniques and concepts of dog training have come a long way in recent times. More and more dog owners and trainers are turning to motivational and fun ways of training their dogs. The concept that the dog must do something, just because 'you said so', is finally becoming the dinosaur approach to training. Harsh methods of general training that include punitive correction are gladly a thing of the past, at least as far as modern forward thinking trainers and owners are concerned.

The method of training described in this booklet works with the dog rather than entering into a battle against it. It takes on board the natural motivations of the dog and harnesses the dog's desires into a training tool that is productive, safe and fun for both the dog and the trainer.

Once the dog has mastered the basics of this mode of learning he will actively strive to learn more. You will have fun watching him work things out for himself as well as being able to guide him with positive training towards your goal.

Read on, have fun and most of all enjoy your dog. But remember you have many choices - your dog has few - make the right choices for your dog and feel good about the way you train, manage and live with your loyal four-footed friend.

Clicker Training - What Is It All About?

The idea behind clicker training is to teach the dog that, when he hears the sound of the clicker, he knows that a reward, (usually food, but it could be anything the dog really values) is coming. This then becomes a very clear, precise and stable signal to the dog, that the behaviour he has given has been the one required and it will be rewarded - he is then much more likely to try to repeat the good behaviour in order to gain the reward. The clicker becomes such a good signal to the dog that, as he develops the skills, it would seem that he works to hear the sound of the clicker alone. You will reach a stage when less reward is needed as the behaviours and the system of training becomes self-rewarding. This is because the dog is having so much fun working with you.

The system is based on the work of a number of behavioural scientists but in particular, on the theories of the scientist B.F. Skinner. It was developed for bird and animal training for the military during the Second World War. Later, in the 1960's it was used in dolphin training and was found to be a most effective 'hands off' style of training.

In more recent times animal trainers world-wide have found it to be an effective system for all manner of training. Its more scientific name is 'successive approximation', often referred to as 'shaping', because the art is in shaping, or progressing a behaviour, nearer and nearer to the required goal.

In 1984 Karen Pryor, a well-respected dolphin trainer, wrote a book that has since become one of the most popular books on operant conditioning. Despite its title, 'Don't Shoot The Dog!' it was not primarily written for dog trainers. However, dog trainers across the world took the book to their hearts because it provided a much-needed path to more humane motivational and enjoyable style of dog training.

What Is A Clicker?

The clicker is a small, plastic, rectangular box. It is fitted with a metal tongue that makes the characteristic 'click' sound when it is depressed. Some trainers may recall having clicker toys as children; the clicking frog was a favourite from my childhood. During wartime the clicker was used to identify friend from foe.

If you don't have a clicker, you could use any sound, the click of a retractable ballpoint pen for example. If you prefer to use a word, signal or different sound, you can still apply the psychology and behavioural training system. In choosing an alternative to the clicker you should work on getting a sound or signal that can be easily repeated, stable in its signal, and readily available for your training sessions. The use of a special word is okay; I have even heard trainers making a verbal clicking noise themselves, but most trainers find that the clicker gets over a much clearer message than the voice.

Clickers are now available from a number of sources including specialist pet shops, trade stands at shows, by mail (address at the back of this book). (Photo J Midgely)

What Does The Clicker Mean To The Dog?

At first, the sound of the clicker means nothing to the dog. He may have an interest in its sound, but once he is conditioned to understand what the sound implies, he will actively work towards discovering and performing the behaviours that produce the click and hence lead to a good reward.

You can use this method of training on any breed (Photo M White)

He will learn that:

(1) The sound 'marks' the aspect of a behaviour that you require and therefore wish to reinforce by reward. It is rather like taking a photograph to catch the precise behaviour wanted. The clicker is sometimes referred to as a 'bridge', i.e. the clicker becomes the bridge between the action and the reward and allows the dog to understand the link between the two.

(2) The sound means that what he has just done is correct and will be rewarded.

(3) The click can mark the end of the behaviour, i.e. the dog learns to come for his reward when he hears the click. In this instance the clicker is known as a 'terminating bridge'.

(4) The click can also mean 'that's good, keep going'. This tends to become the case in more advanced training or when the clicker is used to reinforce, improve and encourage behaviours or exercises already taught. In this instance the clicker is known as an 'intermediate bridge'.

You will not have to continue clicking on every behaviour forever. The clicker is meant to be a training tool and so can be used less and less as the dog learns what is wanted and only introduced when teaching new behaviours, or when you wish to sharpen, re-establish or fine tune behaviours already taught.

Who Uses Clicker Training?

Training using positive reinforcement makes you a very positive and focused trainer. This is because you have to think out what you are going to reinforce. It can be quite difficult to start with, particularly (strangely enough) for some more experienced trainers but, if you think back to how you first started in general dog training, that was quite hard too.

The sorts of people who find clicker training very useful are those with an open mind and a lot of patience. It is perhaps not so easy for the well seasoned trainer to get to grips with, because what he or she already knows and has become accustomed to doing, will interfere with this differing approach.

If you are accustomed to other styles of training but want to have a go, it is best to begin with an exercise not associated with your sport or discipline. This will give you time to understand how the system works, before incorporating it into your training for competition or work.

You will also find that you can train other animals using this system, it even works on husbands, wives and children too! I know of one teacher who actually clicker trains her human pupils! Using this system you can train any animal to do anything, on cue, that it is physically and mentally capable of.

Cats are often said to be un-trainable. If you have a cat have go using this system – you may be pleasantly surprised at the results. This is Jade, a rescue cat who was trained for numerous activities using clicker and target training.
(Photo by John Midgley)

Why Not Just Use Treats or Verbal/Physical Reward

In more traditional styles of training, before the use of conditioned reinforcers such as clickers, it was imperative that the reward came at the time the dog performed the correct act. Of course this is still the case unless you condition your dog.

With conditioned reinforcer training, e.g. clicker training, it does not matter what the dog is doing when he gets his treat, because the message that the dog was correct comes with the click and, once conditioned correctly, he will connect good behaviour with the sound of the click. The click carries the message 'You are right' and it effectively buys you time.

You can give extra treats if you are especially pleased or if the dog has made a good progression, but one single click will get the message over, if it comes at the exact time of the desired act.

It is important with all training to keep it enjoyable for both you and the dog. Therefore, make sure that at every session, you put in some easy exercises to help give the dog confidence and keep his interest and motivation levels high.

Why Use A Clicker?

The reason for using the clicker is that it takes away any need for compulsion in training, there is no need for physical manipulation of the dog. It motivates the animal to be responsive, keen and attentive. There is no place and no need for physical or verbal punishment, the behaviours are 'shaped' using positive reinforcement. You can even discipline an animal using this system (this will be explained later).

One could pose the question, 'Why not just use toys, food or simply praise, why do we need a clicker?' Following are some of the very good reasons in favour of using of the clicker:

1 - Dogs trained with titbits or toys only, tend to nuzzle at the handler's pockets, trying to get to the rewards. Many handlers stop using the rewards because they find that their dog is not concentrating on the job in hand, he is obsessed by the reward and so does not learn very quickly. The clicker tends to get over this problem because the dog is using his ears not his eyes or nose to detect his reward.

2 - Working at a distance to give confidence. It is a great training aid for working at a distance. The animal can be reinforced without the need to rush over to give food, stroke the dog, physically play or throw a toy.

3 - Another problem associated with exercises such as sendaway and scent involving control at a distance is that, the dog tends to look at the handler a lot, this slows down the teaching process. With clicker training the dog can be reinforced while he is facing away from you.

4 - A clicker always sounds the same. Using praise words such as 'good dog' is okay, but praise words can have varying sounds, depending on your mood. They do not always have a clear message for the dog and, of course we use words too much. 'Good dog', amongst the stream of chat, does not stand out but, a clicker, once it is conditioned, will get an instant positive response.

5 - Timing - Another benefit of using the clicker is its split second timing. It is far easier (once practiced) to click than it is to give food, toy or even use a praise word. Therefore, you can use it at the exact time the dog is doing what you want; this is ideal for the inch by inch accuracy needed in sports like competitive obedience training.

For example, the dog comes to the handler for a present position (sitting in front of the handler). The ideal is very neat and straight, but in reality the dog is often crooked. You can decide to reinforce the correct position by use of your clicker, only when he is straight. However, if a straight present does not happen often enough, you can start further back and reinforce the presents that are better than others, and then work towards getting them better by not reinforcing the lesser quality presents, working in a progression towards the perfect present.

Implications For Competition

One of the misconceptions in obedience training is that handlers automatically assume that the clicker is an 'attention getter', but this is not what the system is all

Clicking on near positions can shape a closer present. Ignoring or giving a 'try again' command for others will gradually extinguish the undesirable present positions like this one. (Photo M White)

about. The clicker must be conditioned and trained to be affective. If used indiscriminately the dog will soon learn to ignore it.

Some handlers feel that the clicker is no good because it cannot be used in the ring, well of course not but, nor can any other training aid! You will also find that, because of the way the system works, it is easier to dispense with the clicker and its rewards for ring work, than it is the toy in your hand. This is because you can work with the food/reward off your person from the start.

The clicker can be used to shape new exercises or behaviours and to put the polish on exercises already taught. Of course once they have a good understanding of the system, clever trainers can think up their own conditioned reinforcers that are not visible or audible in the ring!

The Rewards (Primary Reinforcers)

Throughout this booklet I will refer to the reward as food. This is because most trainers use food for clicker training. It is easy to dispense and the vast majority of dogs will respond to some kind of food reward. This is your 'primary reinforcer'. However, it is also possible to use other primary reinforcers such as toys, play or whatever the dog really likes - I conditioned one of my dogs using touch as the reward because that was thing she wanted above all else. As you progress you will find the dog easier to motivate because the whole procedure will become self motivating.

It is best to put the food into a tin, box or pouch, ideally off your person. I find it best to put my training treats in a container and place them on the table or chair so that both the dog and I can see them, but I can control them.

Caution is needed if the dog has a tendency to gain weight. The food should be considered within the total food allowance for the day, therefore it might be necessary to feed less at meal times.

Most dogs will enjoy some form of treat: baked liver, roast chicken, beef, cheese, liver cake, (see the recipe at the end of the booklet). Of course you can use manufactured dog treats too. Try a selection and find a treat that your dog really enjoys and this will enhance his interest. It is a good idea to have a selection of treats, so that some favourite treats can be reserved for extra effort.

The titbits should be very small so that 20 or so repetitions will not leave your dog feeling full.

Where Do Commands Fit In?

Using a clicker helps you to get the behaviour you want, by allowing the dog to learn rather than being manipulated into the action. You should put the commands in, once the dog has learnt the action, then he will not get the incorrect association with the word. If you put in words before the behaviour is perfected, the dog may be learning a completely different association. For example if you continually say the word 'sit' but, achieve only a stand, he may think that sit means stand! (But then this applies whatever training method or principle you choose).

Words used should be clear to the dog. They should be said in a friendly manner – not aggressive or harsh. Try to avoid similar sounding words for differing actions as this may confuse the dog. You should also avoid commands that sound like the dog's name and visa versa.

You also need to consider the desired end result – will the command have to be used with the dog at a distance? If so, then you need to consider how it will sound at that distance and whether you can still call the word in a loud voice – it is not always as easy as you may think. Some words are difficult to call in a loud voice because of the vowel sounds. Practice before you decide what to use.

You must also consider whether the tone will change when adding volume for distance work. If so will the dog still understand that you mean the same thing?

You may wish to consider using signals instead of commands, in some instances this will be better. For example when working outside with the wind against you or in the TV studio when silence is required.

How To Use A Clicker

Getting to grips with a clicker is fun. It will not spoil any training you have already done, and will only take a few minutes of your time. Clickers are very inexpensive to buy, so it is worth giving them a try and it won't break the bank if you decide that you are not going to use it in the future.

Occasionally you will find a dog that is worried by the sound of the clicker. If you have a sound sensitive dog, muffle the sound of the clicker by cupping it in your hand, your pocket or holding it behind your back until the dog comes to realise that the sound has a good connection. You can get clickers with a variable level of sound. In extreme cases it may be necessary to sound the clicker well away from the dog while he is happily playing with you. You could even use a recording to desensitise very sensitive dogs. It is a good idea to sound the clicker every time you feed your dog but again, remember to muffle the sound to begin with. In all cases do not hold the clicker close to the dog's head or ears - try it on your own hearing to see how loud it sounds.

Below is a step by step training routine. However, you should remember to not go on for too long. Always stop while the dog is still interested and hungry.

Step one - Arm yourself with a clicker, a supply of very palatable titbits in a container and a hungry dog.

Step two - Now you need to teach the dog what the click means, and that it means the same wherever you are. To begin with give a click, (just once) and give the dog a treat. Repeat this until it is clear that the dog is making a connection. Lots of dogs achieve this very quickly (within 10 clicks). Others will take longer, maybe a few minutes or even

Start by getting the dog used to what a clicker means, i.e. 'When you hear the sound of the click – food is coming.'
(Photo M White)

a few sessions. Just like us, dogs are all different so keep going, the dog will get the idea sooner or later, assuming the reward is interesting to him. A good test that he is making some association between the clicker and the reward is, if he is looking away and looks back to the food when you click.

Step three - If you were to continue giving rewards every time, the dog would not have to work hard to get his reward, and therefore would cease to try very hard. So the next step is to space the timing of the reward a little, this is called randomising. To do this, click, wait a few seconds, and then reward. Next do the same, but add a few more seconds and reward. Then click and reward immediately. The secret is to not be predictable. Once you have reached the stage where you click and the dog looks attentively at you, in any circumstance or environment, you know the clicker has become a 'conditioned reinforcer'. You can now start to use it to train, reinforce or 'shape' a behaviour.

Step four - To start the training, it is a good idea to train a fun exercise, because although the exercise is not important, it helps you to relax and learn. You have a choice of how to go about this:

(a) Find a way to get a behaviour to occur naturally.
Put the dog in a situation where you know he will give you a behaviour without your interference.
Or

(b) Wait for a behaviour to occur naturally.
For example, the dog may take up a position of his own accord.
Or

(c) Induce the dog into doing something.
You could use a titbit up over his head to induce a sit.
Or

(d) Use something the dog already knows and build on it.
For example, if the dog already knows the down position you could use this to develop a roll over.

When the dog is doing what you want, or is working towards it, click. It is important to click when the dog is actually doing what you want, not before or after. Remember you cannot expect the finished exercise straight away. For example, if teaching a roll over from a down, the first step to click on is the down, next a slight movement to one side, then a little more and so on. Once a progression has been made, stop clicking on lesser behaviours. Keep working on this step until the behaviour seems to be stable and complete.

Step five - To extend the duration or gain the repetition of a behaviour, withhold the click for extended times or until the

The lure can be used to bring the dog into the sit position. (Photo J Midgely)

14

dog has given you more than one repetition of the behaviour but, build up by the second for the best results.

Step six - Continue to click on good behaviours but randomise the reward. The click becomes motivational in itself, but if you cease to reward completely the behaviours may go too.

You can occasionally click without reward, but only when the dog is highly motivated by the behaviour.

If you have trained using treats before, you will now be giving less food than you used to do, it will be more controlled and your dog's performance should have actually improved.

It is a good idea to start by teaching a fun exercise that you are not relying on for competition or work. This way you will not be worried if you do not get it right the first time. This dog gave this behaviour quite easily and naturally – an ideal behaviour to put under cue.
(Photo J Midgely)

Getting Behaviours Under Cue (Command, signal or sound)

The word 'cue' is the technical jargon used for the command, signal or sound you use to trigger the behaviour, e.g. the word 'sit', once trained, becomes the cue for the dog to take up the sit position. It's like taking your cue on stage. The basic principle of getting things under cue is simple.

The cue should be given once only and presented in a clear, precise, non-threatening manner. Each time the cue is given, it should be identical. This is sometimes more difficult when moving from training to working at a distance or in competition, demonstration or work – but in order for the dog to have a clear understanding of what is required, the cue introduced in training must be progressed to the performance later. Therefore, you should give thought to what the cue will be and how it will be given, before you start.

Step one - Develop the behaviour that you want by using the clicker as a conditioned reinforcer as discussed in the previous section. You should be reasonably sure of achieving the behaviour every time before putting it on the cue.

Once you have this, give a word, sound or signal that will mean you want that behaviour to occur and, at the same time induce the desired behaviour. For example say 'sit' and lure the dog with a titbit into a sit. Click as the dog sits. To be sure the dog understands, you should achieve 20 - 40 correct repetitions (over time) in a variety of environments.

Step two - Once you can do this you should cease to click for the behaviour unless it occurs when you have given the command or signal, this way the command or signal becomes 'the cue'.

The behaviour will then become less attractive to the dog, unless he is given the command or signal, to do it, i.e. he will want to do the behaviour 'on cue'. After this the other occurrences of the behaviour will dwindle down to the naturally occurring level although he may go through his repertoire when trying to fathom out a new task.

You can get the dog to hold the position by withholding the click and extending the time lapse second by second.
(Photo M White)

Training With Distractions

Teaching the dog in a quiet environment to begin with is a good idea. It is also a good idea for the dog to be familiar with the environment when he is learning something new. However, once this is reliable you need to introduce him to distractions. You can introduce some distractions yourself, perhaps clapping, dropping something or coughing etc. Initially you may have to give highly palatable rewards to keep his attention, even though you may not have needed these in your initial training.

Introduce distractions as gradually as possible. It is best to keep your distance from the distractions to start. Later, progressing nearer and nearer as the dog's confidence grows.

Work on the very basic elements first, before trying out any more complicated behaviours.

Distraction also comes in the form of a new environment to train in. When first changing training venues, allow the dog time to investigate his new surroundings. This investigation is normal behaviour to the dog – it allows the dog to identify the fact that he is not at risk from predators etc.

In working on the training with changes of venue and distractions, you are teaching the dog to 'generalise' the behaviour. Eventually he will give the behaviour despite the changes.

Another form of generalising is getting the dog to give the behaviour with slightly differing circumstances. For example if he gives you a paw - work on him giving the paw to something else - onto a stick, onto a chair or even to another person. Here he is giving the same behaviour but you are helping him to understand the true meaning even when the circumstances change a little.

Telling The Dog He Is Wrong

You can actually develop a signal to the dog that tells him when he is wrong and, as a consequence, he will not be reinforced. The words 'no', 'try again', 'opps' or 'wrong' could be used. Each time the dog does something other than what you want you could give a negative word or signal that is never rewarded. This word should not sound hard or angry, but should be a simple signal to tell the dog that he is not correct and should try again. Consider the word you use carefully - if you have used the word 'no' in a harsh manner in the past, then it is not the best word to used in this instance.

Time Out!

Occasionally a dog will not respond in the correct way to something he has already learned. Before doing anything about this, you should be sure that the dog has disobeyed, rather than simply misunderstood. It should be remembered that distractions, new environments, and even minor changes in you can confuse the dog and lead to incorrect behaviours. If this could be the case simply start again at the beginning and guide the dog through the procedure.

However, if the dog really does disobey, the worst punishment is to withdraw totally, taking your training treats with you. Give your dog and yourself time to cool off, and then start again repeating the command or signal given previously. Usually this gives a quick response. Withdrawal can be repeated if the dog is still disobeying, but most dogs are devastated by the lack of handler and rewards and really try to comply, if they truly understand the cue.

Extending Exercises

As stated earlier some more experienced dogs can learn that the sound of the clicker is an intermediate bridge and means 'keep going - what you are doing is good'. However, more often the click will signal the end of a behaviour (terminating bridge) and the dog will come back for his reward when he hears the sound. Therefore, it is a good idea to establish a signal that means 'keep going'. Often gentle praise, or a food reward without the click will tell the dog that he is correct and to continue. Another way is to repeat the command as you click. Start with an easy exercise such as sit, and work close to the dog so that you can keep the dog sitting using your training aids. You should then introduce a terminating signal and/or command. Use this command along with a procedure that will break the position. For example, introduce the command 'that'll do' and move the dog off the spot by putting your hand in this collar and easing him onto his feet. You probably don't need to reward this behaviour much as it is self-rewarding, but you can click on it in the intial stages. Once the dog is getting the idea, you will be able to do it without the contact.

Without a signal that the exercise is finished, the dog will make up his own mind and this may not coincide with your ideas! A good clear signal will leave the dog feeling confident and motivated and will give you better overall control.

Some Old Rules Still Apply

Like all training you should not go on for long periods of time. For most dogs little and often is best, with lots of variation. However, too much variation can lead to muddling – be careful to read your dog and attain the right balance. You may find that you reach a point when little progress is being made, this is the same in all learning and is called a 'plateau'. Just keep going you will find success is around the corner.

If the dog starts to go wrong simply go back to basics and start all over again. It is far easier and less confusing for you and the dog, than trying to correct problems. Dogs trained by correction can stand out, because they often do things incorrectly and then correct themselves believing that this is what the handler wants. Be careful that the dog does not think that parts of the shaping process are meant to be in the end product.

If you are training more than one dog, they need to be controlled so that they can't interfere with or distract each other during training. It is best if they are not in the same room or area, at least to start with. However, once the dogs are

If the dog goes wrong, think about why. In most cases it is best to go back to basics to get the dog into the right frame of mind. (Photo M White)

competent, working in front of each other may make them more keen to come training. If they are in the same area, put them in a crate or tie them up. If they become too noisy or obviously distressed, it is best to put them out of sight and hearing of the training until you can work on this issue as a part of the training process - you may need help for this.

If you make a mistake just play with the dog, smile and start again. Alternatively, go and have a cup of tea and come back to training when you have 'got your act together'.

Clicker Training In Dog School

Many trainers worry about their dog's reaction to other people's clickers. However, you will find that this is not normally a problem. Even in a class full of handlers all using a clicker, the dog very quickly comes to understand which click is his, ignoring all others in favour of the sound of his own handler's clicker.

Some very sound sensitive dogs can become distracted, especially if indoors in a room that echoes - if this is the case it is better to allow the dog time to get used to the noise by sitting on the side lines for a while.

Condition the dog at home or in an environment where there are no distractions. Don't try to introduce something new in an environment that is distracting. Once he is very confident, introduce him into smaller groups to start with. It is perhaps better to start outside where the acoustics will not play a part in confusing your dog's very sensitive hearing.

It may be better to start outside when training clicker in a group
(Photo A White)

Target Training

Target training is generally seen as an offshoot of clicker training. However it can be used on its own. Used in conjunction with the clicker training concept it works very well. A target is simply something the dog learns to touch or follow. Your fingers can be a target to the dog, especially in exercises where the dog follows your hand. However, your hand does many other things and using it as a target can be confusing unless you are very careful and focused.

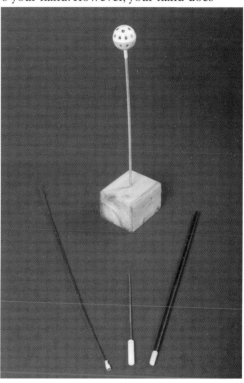

Most trainers use a wooden stick painted black on the main body but with a white tip, rather like a magic wand. Alternatively you could use a telescopic lecture stick, put a little white electrical tape on the end to make the end stand out. In the absence of any of these you can use a piece of wood from a tree. The stick should not be too long, about 2 feet (60cm) maximum and around 1/4 inch (10-12 cm) diameter.

The dog is taught to touch the end and then, this becomes a very positive target that can be used to encourage the dog into correct positions or places, to train or perfect a variety of exercises/behaviours.

The dog can be taught to target to other items too. A spot or mat on the ground is a good way of teaching the dog to go to a set point. The beam of torch is especially useful for those with mobility problems.

Left to right – the first stick is a telescopic lecture's stick, ideal to slip in your pocket and always have available for impromptu training sessions. Next is a simple metal rod with a white tip. Next is a painted wooden dowel with a white tip. At the back is a spring like stick with a cat ball on the top, mounted on a wooden block so that it can be free standing for training at a distance.
(Photo J Midgely)

21

Teaching The Dog To Target

Step one - The dog must be taught that when he is correct he will get a reward, clicker training is the ideal way. As with normal clicker training, you may find it better to have your rewards in a pot, away from your person so that the dog is not simply watching your hands for the food. If you have already conditioned the dog in this way, he will find this next progression easier to comprehend.

Step two - Hold out the stick, many dogs will immediately go towards it because it is new and interesting. Click as soon as his nose touches the stick (it is usually best to hold the clicker in the same hand as the target stick but, be careful as the vibration/sound travelling down the stick may worry some dogs). If he is not interested be patient, move the stick around a little, and tease with the reward. You can click any movement towards the stick and/or touches near to where you want the dog and then, shape

Most dogs will investigate a new object put in front of them! Be ready to click when the dog goes towards the stick.
(Photo M White)

towards the right place, as you would shape other behaviours. To start with it does not matter if the dog touches the main body of the stick or even attempts to hold it, click on any move towards the right behaviour. Keep repeating until the dog has made a connection.

Step three - Move the stick away from the dog a little and continue to reward each time he touches the stick, ignore any other behaviours. If he gives the stick a good or very positive touch give extra rewards. He will now have to actively move to the stick.

Step four - Once you feel the dog has the idea, introduce a targeting cue word, for example 'touch'. Say this word as he touches, and then later when you invite him to touch. When he touches click and reward.

Step five - Cease to reward any touches that are off cue.

Step six - Generalise by changing the environment.

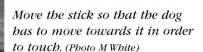

Move the stick so that the dog has to move towards it in order to touch. (Photo M White)

Step seven - Use the stick to encourage a behaviour. A good one to try is to get the dog to put his paws up on to something. Start with the stick within easy reach and then gradually move it back so that the dog must reach forward and finally get his paws up in order to touch.

When the dog gives a very positive touch - give extra or better rewards
(Photo M White)

Brontë does 'Paws up' to her favourite target stick. This easily shapes to the dog on a table etc. (Photo M White)

Step eight - Get the new behaviour under cue. 'Paws up'. Gradually hold the stick in place for shorter periods as the dog's confidence grows in the new command.

Step nine - you can now teach the dog to 'touch' other objects too. Once this is done you can have a variety of targets with a wide ranging number of applications. Put the target stick onto the item and encourage the dog to touch the two together, then as the dog becomes confident, connect a word to the item and then gradually, withdraw the original target stick. This will leave the dog targeting to the new item.

Application Examples for Targeting

Targeting can be used for all manner of training for competitions. Below are some of the aspects that handlers have found particularly useful:

Agility Training

Using the target to encourage the dog to go where you want him, the dog begins to learn for himself, how to master the various apparatus. This is far better than the handler having to physically manipulate the dog.

Contact Equipment - The dog follows the target over the contact points (lower, differently coloured part of A frame, dog walk and seesaw). You could also use a flat object as the target on the contacts, a plastic lid for example.

Use the target stick to encourage the dog to the end of the contacts on the dog walk, A frame and seesaw. (Photo J Midgely)

Jumps - Point to the centre of a tyre jump, above the bar on a hurdle or just beyond the long jump and then pull the target away as the dog gains in confidence. You can adjust the amount of lift and length of stride by sensible positioning of the target stick.

Table - The target stick is a great way to shape the dog's behaviour to get him onto the table. Start at the edge. The dog will rise up to touch the target. Then, gradually draw the stick towards the centre and later, a little beyond, to get the dog into the centre of the table.

Weave - The dog follows the stick through the weave.

A gradual progression will result in a confident relaxed table exercise. (Photo J Midgely)

25

Competitive Obedience Training

Heelwork - The dog follows the target to perfect the desired heel position. You can start with the stick held out at arms length and then gradually bring it in closer to your side. Ultimately, hold the stick so that the end is just beyond the position that you want the dog to hold his head. You can also work on the dog's gait by having him trotting around at arm's length to the target, and then

Teach a touch to the hand
when you are happy with the gait, put a name to it then bring this closer and closer to the heel position.

Instead of (or as well as) using the target stick you can also teach the dog to target to the hand for heelwork, especially with medium or larger dogs. (See photo sequence).

Recall - The target is held in front of the handler, (or to heel for the moving recall), to encourage the dog into the correct present or heel position.

Then bring the hand into the heel position – guiding the dog in with it

26

You can also use your fingers as the target, hold them in the right place to get the dog to come to the centre of your body for the present or in the heel position for the recall to heel.

Retrieve - The dog can be shaped to retrieve from the beginning, by teaching the touch and then shaping a gradual progression. Rewarding a touch, then open mouthed touch, then hold and so on. The

As the dog gets the idea gradually raise the hand – use your touch command to maintain the position

behaviour can then be placed under cue. Next it can be generalised to other articles by starting at the beginning again. The dog will learn rapidly on new articles if you start at the beginning each time.

Scent - To hold a scent cloth or article correctly. The dog's behaviour can be shaped in the same was as described for retrieve.

Over time raise the hand to the correct position (Photo sequence J Midgely)

27

A sendaway to a cone is a common obedience test. It is made simple by using targeting. Train the dog to the target and add the down (UK obedience) or stand (FCI obedience) later when the dog has a strong desire to go to the cone. (Photo J Midgely)

Sendaway - The target is stuck in, or placed on the ground and the previously conditioned dog readily goes to the target by using your touch command. Distance is built up gradually. Targets can be varied to cover the diverse range of sendaway markers. The dog can also be trained to ignore other targets and go for the named target. This will help the dog to go through position/box markers to a back marker.

Working Trials

Tracking - The target stick is drawn along the desired track, the dog picks up the scent and follows the track. Dogs that are accustomed to following the target stick will transfer the skill very quickly to using their nose on the track and finding objects. The target can also be used to shape a pick up of articles for tracking, searching and the standard retrieve.

Agility section - as in agility the dog can be guided by use of the stick over the jumps, up and down the scale etc.

Target and clicker can be used to get a stable hold and retrieve exercise (Photo T Gube)

Obedience section - The obedience side of trials can be encouraged by this very motivational style of training. A natural style can be enhanced to achieve the stability that ensures the dog gaining maximum points by getting clear messages to the dog when he is correct. *(See Competitive Obedience Training)*

Heelwork To Music/Freestyle

Weave though the legs

The freedom and style of the musical sports makes them ideal for the use of clicker and target within the training. A catalogue of moves and

Circle pole

Synchronised paw and foot lift

exercises make up the best performances. Illustrated are just some of the moves that can be trained using clicker and target training:

Hind leg stand (Photo sequence A White)

Media Training

Teaching your dog to go to a certain spot on set or putting his paws where they are needed couldn't be easier when using targeting. Simply put the target where you want the dog, make it easy to start with by working close or easily within reach and then once the dog has grasped the exercise extend to the required distance.

Teaching your dog to go to a given spot and give a behaviour is made much quicker by using target training. (Photo J Midgely)

Even your cat can be trained for the limelight using this method!
(Photo J Midgely)

Appendix 1

Liver Cake Recipe

Ingredients
2lb liver
2lb flour wholemeal
2 eggs
Milk to bind if necessary
Head of garlic

Method
Liquidise the liver and garlic.
Line a baking tin and pour in mixture.
Bake till set (190°/gas mark 4) approx. 1/2 hour.
Cool; cut into titbit size pieces.
Freeze in usable quantities.

Appendix 2

Book and Booklets Available Direct From Rainbow Publishing
More copies of this booklet
Clicker and Target Training - Teaching for Fun and Competition
Author Angela White. Published by Rainbow, 2003. £4.99 Plus 50p P&P UK
(£1.00 P&P Europe, £1.50 P&P rest of the world)
Order 10 or more copies 10% discount
Other Booklets by Angela White...

How to be top dog
How to recognise, deal with and treat dominant dogs in a domestic
environment. From puppy growls, to viscous attacks, this booklet helps
owners to avoid confrontations and get the behaviour under their own
control.

Home Alone Canine
Getting dogs used to being alone, how to combat stress. Dealing with the
problems owners and their dogs face when they are left alone. Including
chewing, barking, urinating, defecating as well as associated behaviours.

Dog Training
Basic techniques for getting control of your pet. All based on kind,
motivational methods of training that work with the dog's own desires.
Includes: sit, down, stand, come back, walk on a loose lead, leave and don't
jump up.

Above 3 booklets published by Rainbow, 2003. £3.99 inc. P&P UK (£1.00
P&P Europe, £1.50 P&P rest of the world)
Order 10 or more copies 10% discount

Other books by Angela White

Everybody Can Train Their Own Dog,
A-Z of Dog training and behaviour problems for all dogs owners. Endorsed by a founder member of the British Institute of Professional Dog Trainers, and with the ASPCA seal of approval, this easy to follow book gives advice in a handy, fully illustrated format. A must for every dog owner.
Published 1992 TFH. ISBN 0-86622-524-2

Happy Dogs Happy Winners (Revised Edition Published 2003)
Complete manual of obedience training. Endorsed by top obedience champion handlers, this book is ideal for complete beginners and more experienced handlers alike. Each exercise is covered with a step by step approach to enable the discerning trainer to work their way from the beginner class right through to championship level competition.
First published 1993 Rainbow Publishing. Second revised edition 2003, Rainbow Publishing. ISBN 1-899057-00-5
Price £12.95 Plus £1.50 P&P UK, (£2.90 P&P rest of the world).
First edition available in German Translation Price £14.95 Plus P&P as above.

Puppies Your Successful Guide To Dog Ownership,
This definitive work covers every aspect of puppy care right through to adulthood. How to chose a pet, how to look after it, why it behaves in the way it does, how to train it and much more. This book is not just for new puppy owners but, is an ideal book for all who have interests in dogs.
Published 1997 UK, TFH/Kingdom. ISBN 185279023-7
Price £19.95 Plus £3.00 P&P UK (£4.50 rest of the world)

The Leonberger,
Essential reading for anyone interested in this most majestic of breeds. This spell binding, beautifully illustrated book includes the fascinating history of the breed, how to train using kind, humane, motivational methods, and even the breeding of this giant of the dog world. It is most definitely a user's guide to owning the most magnificent of breeds, the Leonberger.
Published 1998, TFH/Kingdom. ISBN 185279064-4
Price £24.95 Plus £3.00 P&P UK (£4.50 rest of the world)

Dog Training Instructor's Manual
This much acclaimed instructor's 'bible', is a comprehensive book which includes all you need to know to teach others the art of dog training. From setting up a school, organising classes and courses, how to keep the pupils attention and how to conduct yourself. It includes advice on puppy groups, problem dogs, specialist training as well as standard pet dog control.
Published 2000, Rainbow Publishing. ISBN 1-899057-02-1
Price £12.95 Plus £2.00 P&P UK (£2.90 rest of the world)

Appendix 3

Other Items Available

Clickers £2.50 + 30p P&P
Order 10 or more 10% discount
Don't shoot The Dog! Author Karen Pryor
Bantam Books
ISBN 0-553-25388-3

ESSENTIAL READING FOR DOG LOVERS

The Wolf Talk

'Wolf Man' Shaun Ellis launched his first book at Crufts 2003. It is based on his life, living, eating, sleeping and even howling with the wolves. This enchanting, rivetting, thought provoking book will fill you with wonder at his marvellous knowledge. Illustrated with pictures of Shaun's wolves this book is one you will not be able to put down.

Shaun is also available for lectures. UK dog clubs, organisations, colleges or individuals are invited to host a lecture from this very special man.

These unique talks can include: wolf communication and language, daily life within the pack, identifying and reacting to challenges, daily testing according to rank and links to the domestic dog. For those wanting a little more he will cover animal behavioural science and its role in captive and wild animals, maintenance of social structure, scent, sight, husbandry, welfare, housing and much more. To raise public awareness Shaun's enthusiastic account of Myths and legends, effects of wolves on the ecosystem, the affects on livestock, preventing wolf attacks. He will even tell you how to gain a career working with these wonderful creatures.

Order your signed copy of The Wolf Talk by sending a cheque for £12.95 to the address below.

To find out available dates, costs etc. for lectures, contact Angela or Michael White on Telephone/Fax 01427 753918.

Or write to: Rainbow Publishing, PO Box 1044, Haxey, Doncaster. DN9 2JL

Appendix 4

Courses with the author

International Animal Behaviour Training Centre
With Course Leader Angela White
Clicker Training - Learn the art of clicker training direct from Angela, understand its uses, and have fun shaping behaviours for all aspects of training and behaviour control. Send for details or organise your own course through a club, society or training school.

Competitive Obedience - From beginner to C all levels welcome at a 5 day summer school in August. Held at Angela's home, come each day, camp on site, or take up local B&B and enjoy 5 days of competitive obedience training all using motivational and enjoyable techniques.

Correspondence Courses - Open learning in the comfort of your own home and at your own pace. A wide variety of courses to study, full back up given, qualified tutor support.

Qualifications - Angela is involved in the courses at a range of levels from entry to Degree, delivered through Bishop Burton College. Courses include those relating to dog training and behaviour, instructing and also more wide ranging general animal behaviour and training, animal science etc. For more details on individual courses plus dates, prices and booking forms send stamped addressed envelope to the address below.

Author, Course and IABTC leader Angela White can also be booked to teach at your own venue in the UK, Europe and world-wide. Courses can be structured from Angela's vast range of knowledge to meet your needs on training, behaviour and many other areas of animal care.
Contact: Angela or Michael White,
PO Box 1044, Haxey, Doncaster. DN9 2JL.
Tel 01427 753918 (24 hour ansaphone)